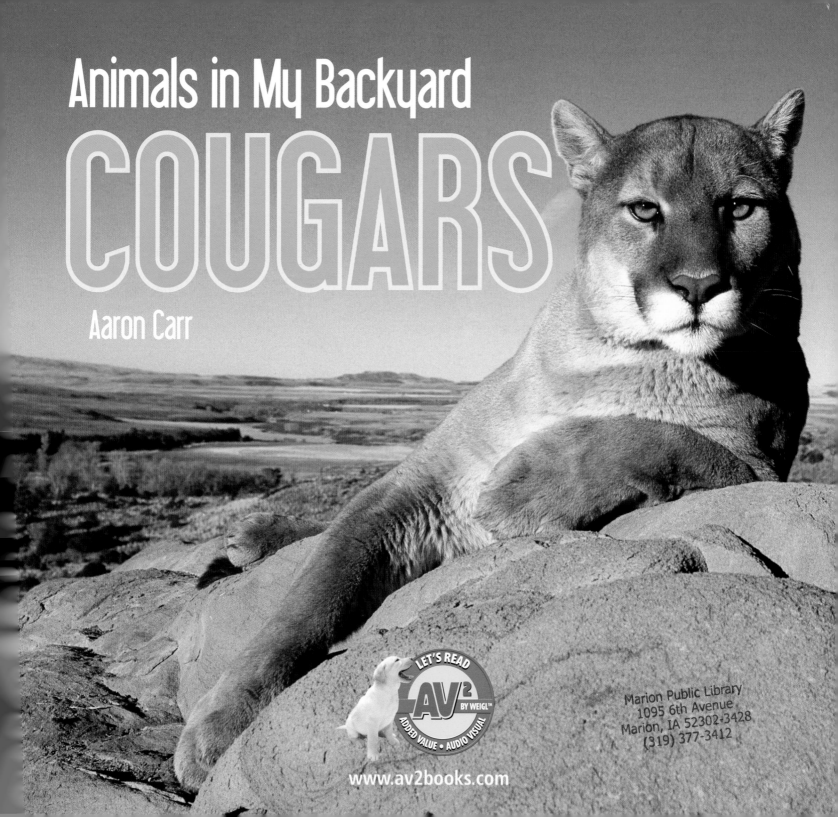

Animals in My Backyard
COUGARS

Aaron Carr

LET'S READ
AV2 BY WEIGL™
ADDED VALUE • AUDIO VISUAL

Go to **www.av2books.com**, and enter this book's unique code.

BOOK CODE

Q999039

AV2 by Weigl brings you media enhanced books that support active learning.

AV² provides enriched content that supplements and complements this book. Weigl's AV² books strive to create inspired learning and engage young minds in a total learning experience.

Your AV² Media Enhanced books come alive with...

Audio
Listen to sections of the book read aloud.

Video
Watch informative video clips.

Embedded Weblinks
Gain additional information for research.

Try This!
Complete activities and hands-on experiments.

Key Words
Study vocabulary, and complete a matching word activity.

Quizzes
Test your knowledge.

Slide Show
View images and captions, and prepare a presentation.

... and much, much more!

Published by AV² by Weigl.
350 5th Avenue, 59th Floor New York, NY 10118
Website: www.av2books.com   www.weigl.com

Library of Congress Cataloguing in Publication data available upon request.
Fax 1-866-449-3445 for the attention of the Publishing Records department.

ISBN 978-1-62127-210-6 (hardcover)
ISBN 978-1-62127-214-4 (softcover)

Printed in the United States of America in North Mankato, Minnesota
2 3 4 5 6 7 8 9 0   17 16 15 14 13

092013
WEP120913

Senior Editor: Aaron Carr   Art Director: Terry Paulhus

Weigl acknowledges Getty Images as the primary image supplier for this title. Page 16: Sebastian Kennerknecht.

Animals in My Backyard
COUGARS

CONTENTS

Meet the cougar.

She is a large cat with brown fur. Her brown fur helps her hide from other animals.

5

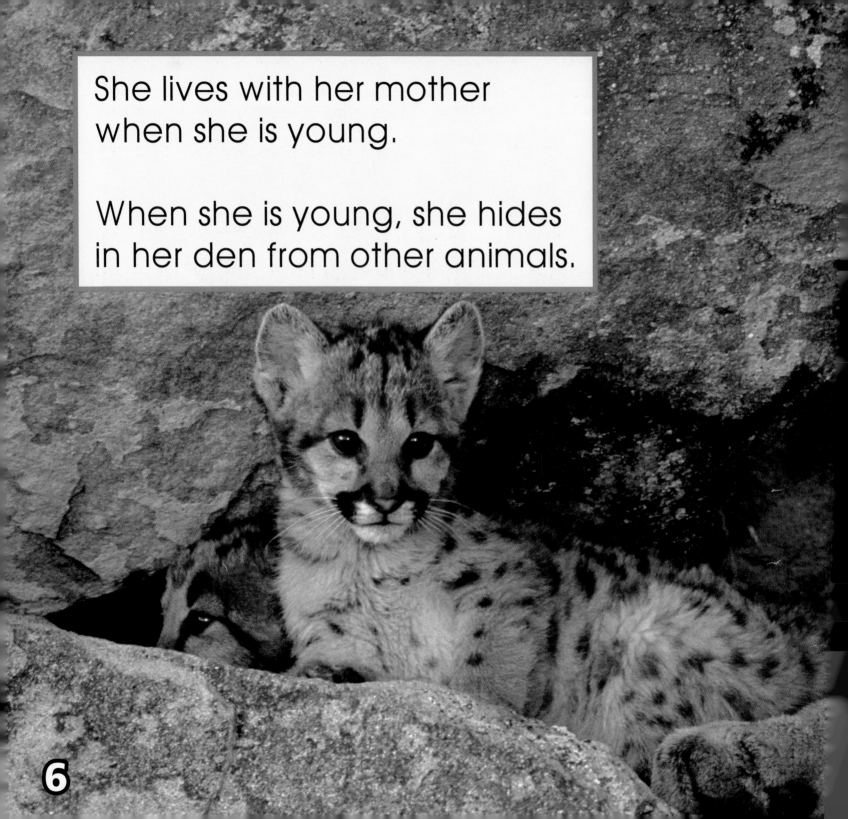

She lives with her mother when she is young.

When she is young, she hides in her den from other animals.

6

She has strong back legs.

With her strong back legs, she can jump 30 feet.

She has a long tail.

With her long tail,
she keeps her balance up high.

She can see well with her eyes.

With her eyes,
she can see in the dark.

She can walk very slowly.

Very slowly, she sneaks up on other animals.

She hunts at night.

At night, she walks up to 6 miles looking for food.

She lives in South and North America.

In South and North America, she lives in forests, swamps, and deserts.

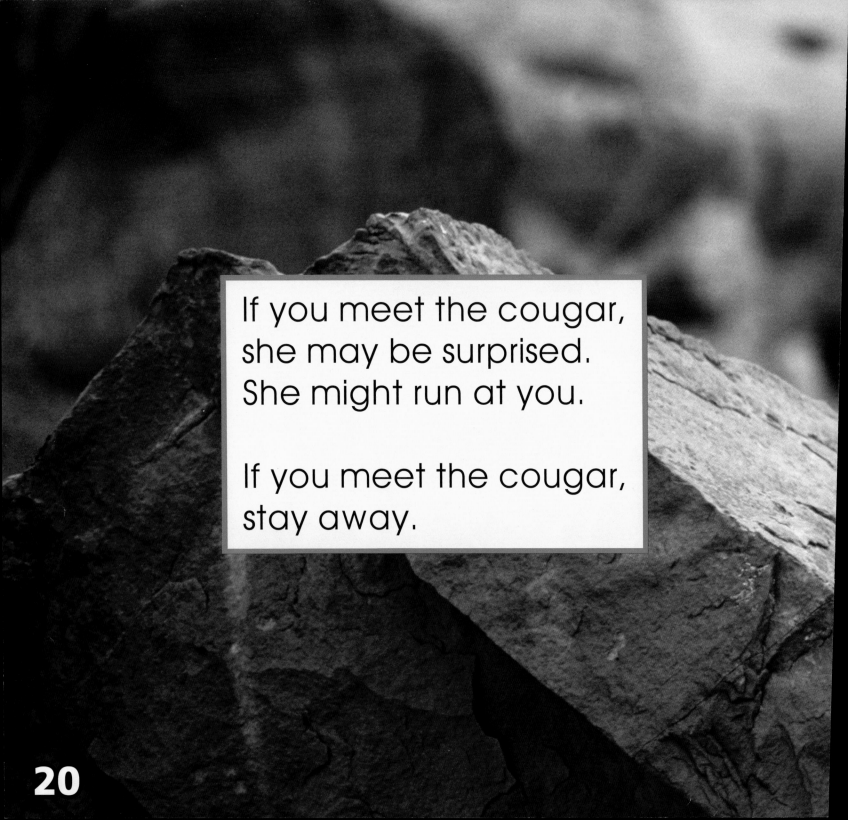

If you meet the cougar, she may be surprised. She might run at you.

If you meet the cougar, stay away.

21

COUGAR FACTS

These pages provide more detail about the interesting facts found in the book. They are intended to be used by adults as a learning support to help young readers round out their knowledge of each animal featured in the *Animals in My Backyard* series.

Pages 4–5

Cougars are large cats with brown fur. The shade of brown can vary from gray to reddish-brown. The cougar usually has white fur around its mouth. It is the second-largest cat species in the western hemisphere. Only the jaguar is bigger. Cougars have been known to grow as large as 220 pounds (100 kilograms). They can be up to 6.5 feet (2 meters) long, including the tail.

Pages 6–7

Cougars live with their mothers when they are young. Cougar mothers may give birth to one to six cubs. The mother raises the cubs by herself. For the first 40 to 70 days after birth, the mother and cubs live in a nesting den. This is often covered by very dense plant cover to keep the cubs hidden. Cubs stay with their mother for 10 to 26 months before leaving to fend for themselves.

Pages 8–9

Cougars have strong back legs. They can use these powerful hind legs to jump 18 feet (5.5 m) straight up in the air. Cougars can also cover a distance up to 30 feet (9 m) in a single jump. Their strong legs are not just used for jumping, however. Cougars have been recorded sprinting at speeds up to 35 miles (56 km) per hour.

Pages 10–11

The cougar has a long tail. A cougar's tail can be about 2.5 feet (0.75 m) long. The tail is also quite thick and heavy compared to other cat species. The cougar uses its long, heavy tail to keep its balance. The tail also works as a counter weight to help the cougar turn quickly while running. Large front paws help with balance as well.

Pages 12–13

Cougars have excellent vision. A cougar's field of vision spans 130 degrees. Like other cats, the cougar's eyes are adapted to seeing at night. There is a reflective layer at the back of the eyes called the *tapetum lucidum* , which means "bright carpet." This reflects light inside the eye to help cougars see better at night. This is why a cougar's eyes appear to shine in the dark.

Pages 14–15

Cougars move slowly and carefully to stalk their prey. They use both stealth and speed when hunting. Cougars first stalk their prey, moving quietly to avoid being seen. The cougar waits until it has a chance to catch its prey. Then, the cougar pounces. It covers distance quickly to catch the prey before it can run.

Pages 16–17

Cougars hunt at night. They prefer to hunt in the dark hours of dusk, night, or dawn. Cougars mostly hunt deer, but they also hunt smaller animals, such as coyotes, raccoons, hares, opossums, and porcupines. Cougars will travel up to 6 miles (10 km) in one night to search for food. In North America, the average cougar hunts 48 deer each year, in addition to many smaller animals.

Pages 18–19

Cougars live in South and North America. They range from Alaska to the southern tip of South America. Cougars have adapted to many habitats, from forests and chaparrals to wetlands and deserts. Cougars are called many different names. In South America, they are called pumas. In parts of the United States, they are known as mountain lions. They are called panthers in Florida.

Pages 20–21

Beware of cougars when out in the wilderness. When people encounter cougars in nature, the cougar could be surprised or afraid. It might attack to protect itself. Cougars usually avoid people. However, there are still reports of attacks every year in the United States and Canada. Most victims are people traveling alone. To avoid an encounter with a cougar, always travel in groups.

KEY WORDS

Research has shown that as much as 65 percent of all written material published in English is made up of 300 words. These 300 words cannot be taught using pictures or learned by sounding them out. They must be recognized by sight. This book contains 46 common sight words to help young readers improve their reading fluency and comprehension. This book also teaches young readers several important content words. These words are paired with pictures to aid in learning and improve understanding.

Page	Sight Words First Appearance
4	the
5	a, animals, from, helps, her, is, large, other, she, with
6	in, lives, mother, when, young
8	back, has
9	can, feet
10	long
11	high, keeps, up
12	eyes, see, well
14	very, walk
15	on
16	at, food, for, looking, miles, night, to
18	America, and
20	away, be, if, may, might, run, you

Page	Content Words First Appearance
4	cougar
5	cat, fur
6	den
8	legs
10	tail
11	balance
13	dark
19	deserts, forests, swamps

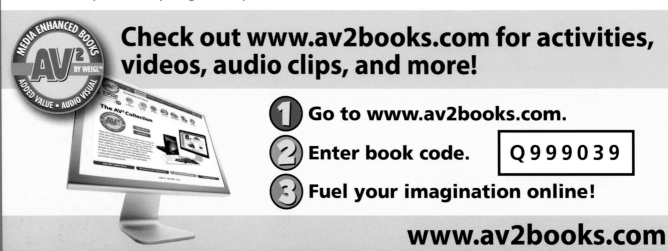

Check out www.av2books.com for activities, videos, audio clips, and more!

1 Go to www.av2books.com.

2 Enter book code. Q999039

3 Fuel your imagination online!

www.av2books.com